TO

_____

FROM

_____

DATE

_____

PRAYERS

of a *Righteous*

Man

FOURTH EDITION

PRAYERS

of a *Righteous*

Man

Cover Design by Kim Russell / Wahoo Designs
Page Layout by Bart Dawson

ISBN 1-58334-245-1

Printed in the United States of America

Table of Contents

Introduction   11

1. The Prayers of a Righteous Man   13
2. Learning the Art of Acceptance   17
3. Walking the Walk   21
4. Beyond Anger   25
5. Beyond Busyness   29
6. A Man of Character   33
7. The Joys of a Clear Conscience   37
My Thoughts & Prayers from This Week   41
My Thoughts & Prayers for Next Week   42
8. A New Creation   43
9. Living Courageously   47
10. Decisions, Decisions, Decisions   51
11. Tackling Tough Times   55
12. Following Christ   59
13. Seeking God's Plan   63
14. Searching for Strength   67
My Thoughts & Prayers from This Week   71
My Thoughts & Prayers for Next Week   72
15. Patience and Trust   73
16. The Steps of a Righteous Man   77

17. A Humble Spirit   81

18. Leadership   85

19. Discovering Time for Prayer
    and Meditation   89

20. Keeping Money in Perspective   93

21. An Obedient Heart   97

My Thoughts & Prayers from This Week   101

My Thoughts & Prayers for Next Week   102

22. The Passionate Believer   103

23. The Power of Perseverance   107

24. Beyond Worry   111

25. Real Repentance   115

26. Seeking God   119

27. God's Sovereignty   123

28. Protection from Temptation   127

My Thoughts & Prayers from This Week   131

My Thoughts & Prayers for Next Week   132

29. Sharing the Good News   133

30. The Value of Hard Work   137

31. The Ultimate Power,
    The Ultimate Love   141

My Thoughts & Prayers for the Month   145

Bible Verses to Consider   147

Introduction

How desperately our world needs Christian men who are willing to honor God with their service. This generation faces problems that defy easy solutions, yet face them we must. We need leaders whose vision is clear and whose intentions are pure. Daniel writes, "Those who are wise will shine like the brightness of the heavens, and those who lead many to righteousness, like the stars for ever and ever" (12:3 NIV). Hopefully, you are determined to be such a man—a man who walks in wisdom as he offers counsel and direction to his family, to his friends, and to his coworkers.

In your hands, you hold a book that contains 31 devotional readings. Each chapter contains Bible verses, a brief essay, inspirational quotations from noted Christian thinkers, and a prayer.

During the next 31 days, please try this experiment: read a chapter each day. If you're already committed to a daily time of worship, this book will enrich that experience. If you are not, the simple act of giving God a few minutes each morning will change the direction and the quality of your life.

Every day provides opportunities to put God where He belongs: at the center of our lives. When we do so, we worship Him, not just with words, but with deeds. And, we become dutiful servants of God, righteous men who share His Son's message of love and salvation with the world. May *you* be that righteous man.

CHAPTER 1

The Prayers of a Righteous Man

I desire therefore that the men pray everywhere,
lifting up holy hands, without wrath and doubting.
1 Timothy 2:8 NKJV

"The power of prayer": these words are so familiar, yet sometimes we forget what they mean. Prayer is a powerful tool for communicating with our Creator; it is an opportunity to commune with the Giver of all things good. Prayer helps us find strength for today and hope for the future. Prayer is not a thing to be taken lightly or to be used infrequently.

Is prayer an integral part of your daily life, or is it a hit-or-miss habit? Do you "pray without ceasing," or is your prayer life an afterthought? Do you regularly pray in the solitude of the early morning darkness, or do you bow your head only when others are watching?

The quality of your spiritual life will be in direct proportion to the quality of your prayer life. Prayer changes things, and it changes you. So today, instead of turning things over in your mind, turn them over to God in prayer. Instead of worrying about your next decision, ask God to lead the way. Don't limit your prayers to meals or to bedtime. Pray constantly about things great and small. God is listening, and He wants to hear from you now.

Prayer accomplishes more than anything else.

Bill Bright

Avail yourself of the greatest privilege this side
of heaven: prayer. Jesus Christ died to make this
communion and communication with
the Father possible.

Billy Graham

Prayer does not change God; it changes me.

C. S. Lewis

The Christian on his knees sees
more than the philosopher on tiptoe.

D. L. Moody

*The effective prayer of a righteous man
can accomplish much.*

James 5:16 NASB

A Prayer for Today

Dear Lord, make me a person whose constant
prayers are pleasing to You. Let me come
to You often with concerns both great and
small. And, when You answer my prayers,
Father, let me trust Your answers,
today and forever.

Amen

CHAPTER 2

Learning the Art of Acceptance

*One thing I do, forgetting those things which are
behind and reaching forward to those things which
are ahead, I press toward the goal for the prize of
the upward call of God in Christ Jesus.*

Philippians 3:13-14 NKJV

If you're like most men, you like being in control. Period. You want things to happen according to *your* wishes and according to *your* timetable. But sometimes, God has other plans . . . and He always has the final word.

The American theologian Reinhold Niebuhr composed a profoundly simple verse that came to be known as the Serenity Prayer: "God, grant me the serenity to accept the things I cannot change, the courage to change the things I can, and the wisdom to know the difference." Niebuhr's words are far easier to recite than they are to live by.

Author Hannah Whitall Smith observed, "How changed our lives would be if we could only fly through the days on wings of surrender and trust!" These words remind us that even when we cannot understand the workings of God, we must trust Him and accept His will.

So if you've encountered unfortunate circumstances that are beyond your power to control, accept those circumstances . . . and trust God. When you do, you can be comforted in the knowledge that your Creator is both loving and wise, and that He understands His plans perfectly, even when you do not.

I am truly grateful that faith enables me
to move past the question of "Why?"

Zig Ziglar

Faith in God will not get for you everything
you want, but it will get for you what God
wants you to have. The unbeliever does not
need what he wants; the Christian should
want only what he needs.

Vance Havner

The more comfortable we are with mystery
in our journey, the more rest
we will know along the way.

John Eldredge

Acceptance is taking from God's hand
absolutely anything He gives, looking into
His face in trust and thanksgiving, knowing
that the confinement of the hedge
we're in is good and for His glory.

Charles Swindoll

> *I have learned to be content whatever the circumstances.*
>
> ↩
>
> *Philippians 4:11 NIV*

A Prayer for Today

Father, the events of this world unfold according to a plan that I cannot fully understand. But You understand. Help me to trust You, Lord, even when I am troubled. Help me to trust You even when I am confused. Today, in whatever circumstances I find myself, let me trust Your will and accept Your love . . . completely.

↩

Amen

CHAPTER 3

Walking the Walk

*But prove yourselves doers of the word,
and not merely hearers who delude themselves.*

James 1:22 NASB

The old saying is both familiar and true: actions speak louder than words. And as believers, we must beware: our actions should always give credence to the changes that Christ can make in the lives of those who walk with Him.

God calls upon each of us to act in accordance with *His* will and with respect for *His* commandments. If we are to be responsible believers, we must realize that it is never enough simply to hear the instructions of God; we must also live by them. And it is never enough to wait idly by while others do God's work here on earth; we, too, must act. Doing God's work is a responsibility that each of us must bear, and when we do, our loving Heavenly Father rewards our efforts with a bountiful harvest.

Do you seek God's peace and His blessings? Then obey Him. When you're faced with a difficult choice or a powerful temptation, seek God's counsel and trust the counsel He gives. Invite God into your heart and act in accordance with His commandments. When you do, you will be blessed today and tomorrow and forever.

Do noble things, do not dream them
all day long.

Charles Kingsley

Action springs not from thought,
but from a readiness for responsibility.

Dietrich Bonhoeffer

Let us not be content to wait and
see what will happen, but give us
the determination to make
the right things happen.

Peter Marshall

The church needs people who are doers of
the Word and not just hearers.

Warren Wiersbe

*Are there those among you who are truly wise
and understanding? Then they should show it
by living right and doing good things with
a gentleness that comes from wisdom.*

James 3:13 NCV

A Prayer for Today

Dear Lord, I have heard Your Word,
and I have felt Your presence in my heart;
let me act accordingly. Let my words and deeds
serve as a testimony to the changes You have
made in my life. Let me praise You, Father,
by following in the footsteps of Your Son,
and let others see Him through me.

Amen

CHAPTER 4

Beyond Anger

But now ye also put off all these;
anger, wrath, malice . . . .

Colossians 3:8 KJV

Anger is a natural human emotion that is sometimes necessary and appropriate. Even Jesus became angry when confronted with the moneychangers in the temple: "And Jesus entered the temple and drove out all those who were buying and selling in the temple, and overturned the tables of the moneychangers and the seats of those who were selling doves" (Matthew 21:12 NASB). Righteous indignation is an appropriate response to evil, but God does not intend that anger should rule our lives. Far from it. God intends that we turn away from anger whenever possible and forgive our neighbors just as we seek forgiveness for ourselves.

Life is full of frustrations: some great and some small. On occasion, you, like Jesus, will confront evil, and when you do, you may respond as He did: vigorously and without reservation. But, more often your frustrations will be of the more mundane variety. As long as you live here on earth, you will face countless opportunities to lose your temper over small, relatively insignificant events: a traffic jam, a spilled cup of coffee, an inconsiderate comment, a broken promise. When you are tempted to lose your temper over the minor inconveniences of life, don't. Turn away from anger, hatred, bitterness, and regret. Turn instead to God. When you do, you'll be following His commandments and giving yourself a priceless gift . . . the gift of peace.

Anger is the noise of the soul;
the unseen irritant of the heart;
the relentless invader of silence.

Max Lucado

When you strike out in anger, you may miss
the other person,
but you will always hit yourself.

Jim Gallery

Unrighteous anger feeds the ego and
produces the poison of selfishness in the heart.

Warren Wiersbe

Don't become angry quickly,
because getting angry is foolish.

Ecclesiastes 7:9 NCV

A Prayer for Today

Dear Lord, when I am angry, I cannot feel
the peace that You intend for my life.
When I am bitter, I cannot sense Your love.
Heavenly Father, keep me mindful that
forgiveness is Your commandment and
Your will for my life. Let me turn away from
anger and instead claim the spiritual abundance
that You offer through the priceless gift
of Your Son Jesus.

Amen

CHAPTER 5

Beyond Busyness

*Live peaceful and quiet lives
in all godliness and holiness.*
1 Timothy 2:2 NIV

Has the busy pace of life robbed you of the peace that might otherwise be yours through Jesus Christ? If so, you are simply too busy for your own good. Through His only begotten Son, God offers you a peace that passes human understanding, but He won't force His peace upon you; in order to experience it, you must slow down long enough to sense His presence and His love.

Time is a nonrenewable gift from God. How will you use it? You know from experience that you should invest some time each day in yourself, but finding time to do so is easier said than done. As a busy Christian, you may have difficulty investing large blocks of time in much-needed thought and self-reflection. If so, it may be time to reorder your priorities.

"First things first" is an adage that's easy to speak but hard to put into practice. Why? Because we live in a demanding world, a world filled with distractions and temptations. And as we try to prioritize our days and our lives, we are confronted by so many people who are expecting so many things from us! But we must never allow ourselves to become so busy that we fail to make time for God.

Remember: this is the day that God has made and that He has filled it with countless opportunities to love, to serve, and to seek His guidance. Seize those opportunities today, and keep seizing them every day that you live. And as a gift to yourself, to your family, and to the world, slow down and claim the inner peace that is your spiritual birthright: the peace of Jesus Christ. It is offered freely; it has been paid for in full; it is yours for the asking. So ask. And then share.

It is common to think that activity in the service of Christ is the indication of the blessing of God, but be aware of barrenness in a busy life.

Franklin Graham

Busyness is the great enemy of relationships.

Oswald Chambers

*The thing you should want most is
God's kingdom and doing what God wants.
Then all these other things you need
will be given to you.*

Matthew 6:33 NCV

A Prayer for Today

Dear Lord, when the quickening pace of life
leaves me with little time for worship or
for praise, help me to reorder my priorities.
When the demands of the day leave me
distracted and discouraged, let me turn to Jesus
for the peace that only He can give. And then,
when I have accepted the spiritual abundance
that is mine through Christ, let me share
His message and His love with
all who cross my path.

Amen

CHAPTER 6

A Man of Character

*Blessed is the man who does not walk in the counsel
of the wicked or stand in the way of sinners or
sit in the seat of mockers. But his delight is in
the law of the LORD, and on his law he meditates
day and night. He is like a tree planted by streams
of water, which yields its fruit in season and whose
leaf does not wither. Whatever he does prospers.*

Psalm 1:1-3 NIV

Charles Swindoll correctly observed, "Nothing speaks louder or more powerfully than a life of integrity." Righteous men—and women—agree.

Character is built slowly over a lifetime. It is the sum of every right decision, every honest word, every noble thought, and every heartfelt prayer. It is forged on the anvil of honorable work and polished by the twin virtues of generosity and humility. Character is a precious thing—difficult to build but easy to tear down. As believers in Christ, we must seek to live each day with discipline, honesty, and faith. When we do, integrity becomes a habit.

If you sincerely wish to be a righteous man, then you must walk with God and you must follow His commandments. When you do, your character will take care of itself . . . and God will surely smile upon you and yours.

Maintaining your integrity in a world of sham is
no small accomplishment.

Wayne Oates

There is no way to grow a saint overnight.
Character, like the oak tree,
does not spring up like a mushroom.

Vance Havner

A solid trust is based on a consistent character.

John Maxwell

Your true character is something
that no one can injure but yourself.

C. H. Spurgeon

In everything set them an example by doing what is good. In your teaching show integrity, seriousness and soundness of speech that cannot be condemned, so that those who oppose you may be ashamed because they have nothing bad to say about us.

Titus 2:7 NIV

A Prayer for Today

Heavenly Father, Your Word instructs me to walk in righteousness and in truth.
Make me Your worthy servant, Lord.
Let my words be true, and let my actions lead others to You.

Amen

CHAPTER 7

The Joys of a Clear Conscience

So I strive always to keep my conscience clear before God and man.

Acts 24:16 *NIV*

When you're about to do something that you know is wrong, a little voice inside your head has a way of speaking up. That voice, of course, is your conscience: an early-warning system designed to keep you out of trouble. If you listen to that voice, you'll be okay; if you ignore it, you're asking for headaches or heartbreaks or both.

Few things in life will torment you more than a guilty conscience. Thankfully, the reverse is also true: a clear conscience is a lasting reward that becomes yours when you know that you've done the right thing.

Whenever you're about to make an important decision, you should listen carefully to the quiet voice inside. Sometimes, of course, it's tempting to do otherwise. From time to time you'll be tempted to abandon your better judgement by ignoring your conscience. But remember: a conscience is a terrible thing to waste. So instead of ignoring that quiet little voice, pay careful attention to it. If you do, your conscience will lead you in the right direction—in fact, it's trying to lead you right now. So listen . . . and learn.

A good conscience is a continual feast.

Francis Bacon

To go against one's conscience is neither
safe nor right. Here I stand.
I cannot do otherwise.

Martin Luther

The voice of the subconscious argues with you,
tries to convince you; but the inner voice
of God does not argue; it does not try
to convince you. It just speaks,
and it is self-authenticating.

C. S. Lewis

God has revealed Himself in man's conscience.
Conscience has been described as
the light of the soul.

Billy Graham

*Let us draw near to God with a sincere heart
in full assurance of faith, having our hearts
sprinkled to cleanse us from a guilty conscience
and having our bodies washed with pure water.*

Hebrews 10:22 NIV

A Prayer for Today

Dear God, You've given me a conscience
that tells me right from wrong.
Let me trust my conscience,
and let me live according to Your teachings,
not just for today, but forever.

Amen

My Thoughts & Prayers
from This Week

_____

_____

_____

_____

_____

_____

_____

_____

_____

_____

_____

_____

_____

_____

_____

_____

_____

_____

_____

_____

_____

_____

My Thoughts & Prayers
for Next Week

CHAPTER 8

A New Creation

Jesus answered and said unto him,
Verily, verily, I say unto thee,
Except a man be born again,
he cannot see the kingdom of God.

John 3:3 KJV

Think, for a moment, about the "old" you, the person you were before you invited Christ to reign over your heart. Now, think about the "new" you, the person you have become since then. Is there a difference between the "old" you and the "new and improved" version? There should be! And that difference should be noticeable not only to you but also to others.

Warren Wiersbe observed, "The greatest miracle of all is the transformation of a lost sinner into a child of God." And Oswald Chambers noted, "If the Spirit of God has transformed you within, you will exhibit Divine characteristics in your life, not good human characteristics. God's life in us expresses itself as God's life, not as a human life trying to be godly."

When you invited Christ to reign over your heart, you became a new creation through Him. This day offers yet another opportunity to *behave yourself* like that new creation. When you do, God will guide your steps and bless your endeavors . . . forever.

How do I know that Jesus has risen?
Because he has risen to the throne of
my own heart. I have seen him work miracles
in my life, one after another, big and small.
He has changed my desires; he has remodeled
my thinking; he has shown me how to love
the unlovable, forgive the unforgivable
(including myself), and move the unmovable
barriers in my path.

Liz Curtis Higgs

Repentance involves a radical change of heart
and mind in which we agree with
God's evaluation of our sin and then take
specific action to align ourselves with His will.

Henry Blackaby

God became man to turn creatures into sons:
not simply to produce better men of
the old kind but to produce a new kind of man.

C. S. Lewis

And He called a child to Himself and set him
before them, and said, "Truly I say to you, unless
you are converted and become like children,
you will not enter the kingdom of heaven."

Matthew 18:2-3 NASB

A Prayer for Today

Lord, when I accepted Jesus as my personal
Savior, You changed me forever and made me
whole. Let me share Your Son's message with
my friends, with my family, and with the world.
You are a God of love, redemption,
conversion, and salvation.
I will praise You today and forever.

Amen

CHAPTER 9

Living Courageously

Be strong and brave, and do the work.
Don't be afraid or discouraged,
because the Lord God, my God, is with you.
He will not fail you or leave you.
1 Chronicles 28:20 NCV

Every human life is a tapestry of events: some grand, some not so grand, and some downright tragic. When we reach the mountaintops of life, praising God is easy. In the moment of triumph, we trust God's plan. But, when the storm clouds form overhead and we find ourselves in the dark valley of despair, our faith is stretched, sometimes to the breaking point. As Christians, we can be comforted: Wherever we find ourselves, whether at the top of the mountain or the depths of the valley, God is there, and because He cares for us, we can live courageously.

Believing Christians have every reason to be courageous. After all, the ultimate battle has already been fought and won on the cross at Calvary. But, even dedicated followers of Christ may find their courage tested by the inevitable disappointments and tragedies that occur in the lives of believers and non-believers alike.

The next time you find your courage tested to the limit, remember that God is as near as your next breath, and remember that He offers salvation to His children. He is your shield and your strength; He is your protector and your deliverer. Call upon Him in your hour of need and then be comforted. Whatever your challenge, whatever your trouble, God can handle it. And will.

The truth of Christ brings assurance and
so removes the former problem
of fear and uncertainty.

A. W. Tozer

Take courage. We walk in the wilderness today
and in the Promised Land tomorrow.

D. L. Moody

Seeing that a Pilot steers the ship in which
we sail, who will never allow us to perish even
in the midst of shipwrecks, there is no reason
why our minds should be overwhelmed with
fear and overcome with weariness.

John Calvin

*Be of good courage, and he shall strengthen
your heart, all ye that hope in the* LORD.

Psalm 31:24 KJV

A Prayer for Today

Dear Lord, sometimes I face disappointments
and challenges that leave me worried and
afraid. When I am fearful, let me seek
Your strength. When I am anxious,
give me faith. Keep me mindful, Lord,
that You are my God. With You by my side,
Lord, I have nothing to fear. Help me
to be Your grateful and courageous servant
this day and every day.

Amen

CHAPTER 10

Decisions, Decisions, Decisions

I have set before you life and death, blessings and curses. Now choose life, so that you and your children may live and that you may love the LORD your God, listen to his voice, and hold fast to him.

Deuteronomy 30:19-20 NIV

L ife is a series of decisions. And the quality of those decisions determines the quality of our lives.

Some decisions are easy to make because the consequences of those decisions are small. When the person behind the counter asks, "Want fries with that?" the necessary response requires little thought because the consequences of that decision are minor. Some decisions, on the other hand, are big . . . *very* big. The biggest decision, of course, is one that far too many people ignore: the decision concerning God's only begotten Son. But if you're a believer in Christ, you've already made that choice, and you have received God's gift of grace. Perhaps now you're asking yourself "What's next, Lord?" If so, you may be facing a series of big decisions concerning your life and your future. Here are some things you can do:

1. **Gather as much information as you can:** Don't expect to get all the facts—that's impossible—but get as many facts as you can in a reasonable amount of time. (Proverbs 24:3-4)

2. **Don't be too impulsive**: If you have time to make a decision, use that time to make a good decision. (Proverbs 19:2)

3. **Rely on the advice of trusted friends and mentors**: Proverbs 1:5 makes it clear: "A wise man will hear and increase learning, and a man of understanding will attain wise counsel" (NKJV),

4. **Pray for guidance**: When you seek it, He will give it. (Luke 11:9)

5. **Trust the quiet inner voice of your conscience**: Treat your conscience as you would a trusted advisor. (Luke 17:21)

6. **When the time for action arrives, act.** Procrastination is the enemy of progress; don't let it defeat you. (James 1:22).

Good and evil both increase at
compound interest. That is why
the little decisions you and I make every day
are of such infinite importance.

C. S. Lewis

The fear of the LORD is the beginning of knowledge, but fools despise wisdom and instruction.

Proverbs 1:7 NKJV

A Prayer for Today

Lord, help me to make decisions that are pleasing to You. Help me to be honest, patient, thoughtful, and obedient. And above all, help me to follow the teachings of Jesus, not just today, but every day.

Amen

CHAPTER 11

Tackling Tough Times

*The Lord says, "Forget what happened before,
and do not think about the past. Look at
the new thing I am going to do. It is already
happening. Don't you see it? I will make
a road in the desert and rivers in the dry land."*

Isaiah 43:18-19 NCV

The occasional disappointments and failures of life are inevitable. Such setbacks are simply the price that we must occasionally pay for our willingness to take risks as we follow our dreams. But even when we encounter bitter disappointments, we must never lose faith.

The words of Hebrews 10:36 remind us of the need for perseverance: "For you have need of endurance, so that when you have done the will of God, you may receive what was promised" (NASB). When we persevere, we will eventually receive that which God has promised. What's required is perseverance, not perfection.

When we encounter the inevitable difficulties of life-here-on-earth, God stands ready to protect us. Our responsibility, of course, is to ask Him for protection. When we call upon Him in heartfelt prayer, He will answer—in His own time and according to His own plan—and He will heal us. And, while we are waiting for God's plans to unfold and for His healing touch to restore us, we can be comforted in the knowledge that our Creator can overcome any obstacle, even if we cannot.

The enemy of our souls loves to taunt us
with past failures, wrongs, disappointments,
disasters, and calamities. And if we let him
continue doing this, our life becomes a long and
dark tunnel, with very little light at the end.

Charles Swindoll

How beautiful it is to learn that grace isn't
fragile, and that in the family of God
we can fail and not be a failure.

Gloria Gaither

If you learn from a defeat,
you have not really lost.

Zig Ziglar

We are either the masters or the victims of
our attitudes. It is a matter of personal choice.
Who we are today is the result of choices we
made yesterday. Tomorrow, we will become
what we choose today. To change means to
choose to change.

John Maxwell

*Let us not become weary in doing good,
for at the proper time we will reap a harvest
if we do not give up.*

Galatians 6:9 NIV

A Prayer for Today

Lord, when life is difficult, I am tempted to
abandon hope in the future. But You are
my God, and I can draw strength from You.
When I am exhausted, You energize me.
When I am fearful, You give me courage.
You are with me, Father, in good times and
in bad times. I will persevere in the work
that You have placed before me,
and I will trust in You forever.

Amen

CHAPTER 12

Following Christ

If anyone serves Me, let him follow Me;
and where I am, there My servant will be also.
If anyone serves Me, him My Father will honor.

John 12:26 NKJV

Jesus loved you so much that He endured unspeakable humiliation and suffering for you. How will you respond to Christ's sacrifice? Will you take up His cross and follow Him (Luke 9:23), or will you choose another path? When you place your hopes squarely at the foot of the cross, when you place Jesus squarely at the center of your life, you will be blessed.

The 19th-century writer Hannah Whitall Smith observed, "The crucial question for each of us is this: What do you think of Jesus, and do you yet have a personal acquaintance with Him?" Indeed, the answer to that question determines the quality, the course, and the direction of our lives today and for all eternity.

The old familiar hymn begins, "What a friend we have in Jesus . . . ." No truer words were ever penned. Jesus is the sovereign friend and ultimate savior of mankind. Christ showed enduring love for His believers by willingly sacrificing His own life so that we might have eternal life. Now, it is our turn to become His friend.

Let us love our Savior, praise Him, and share His message of salvation with our neighbors and with the world. When we do, we demonstrate that our acquaintance with the Master is not a passing fancy; it is, instead, the cornerstone and the touchstone of our lives.

Christ is like a river that is continually flowing. There are always fresh supplies of water coming from the fountain-head, so that a man may live by it and be supplied with water all his life. So Christ is an ever-flowing fountain; he is continually supplying his people, and the fountain is not spent. They who live upon Christ may have fresh supplies from him for all eternity; they may have an increase of blessedness that is new, and new still, and which never will come to an end.

Jonathan Edwards

Our responsibility is to feed from Him, to stay close to Him, to follow Him—because sheep easily go astray—so that we eternally experience the protection and companionship of our Great Shepherd the Lord Jesus Christ.

Franklin Graham

*Then He said to them all,
"If anyone wants to come with Me,
he must deny himself, take up his cross daily,
and follow Me."*

◠

Luke 9:23 HCSB

A Prayer for Today

Dear Lord, You sent Your Son so that I might
have abundant life and eternal life.
Thank You, Father, for my Savior, Christ Jesus.
I will follow Him, honor Him, and share
His Good News, this day and every day.

◠

Amen

CHAPTER 13

Seeking God's Plan

"For I know the plans I have for you,"
declares the LORD, "plans to prosper you and
not to harm you, plans to give you hope and
a future. Then you will call upon me and come
and pray to me, and I will listen to you."

Jeremiah 29:11-12 NIV

God has plans for your life, but He won't force His plans upon you. Your Creator has given you the ability to make decisions on your own. With that freedom comes the responsibility of living with the consequences of your choices.

If you seek to live in accordance with God's plan for your life, you will study His Word, you will be attentive to His instructions, and you will be watchful for His signs. You will associate with fellow believers who, by their words and actions, will encourage your own spiritual growth. You will assiduously avoid those two terrible temptations: the temptation to sin and the temptation to squander time. And finally, you will listen carefully, even reverently, to the conscience that God has placed in your heart.

God has glorious plans for your day and your life. So as you go about your daily activities, keep your eyes and ears open . . . as well as your heart.

It's incredible to realize that what we do each day has meaning in the big picture of God's plan.

Bill Hybels

When the dream of our heart is one that God has planted there, a strange happiness flows into us. At that moment, all of the spiritual resources of the universe are released to help us. Our praying is then at one with the will of God and becomes a channel for the Creator's purposes for us and our world.

Catherine Marshall

The one supreme business of life is to find God's plan for your life and live it.

E. Stanley Jones

When God speaks to you through the Bible, through prayer, through circumstances, through the church, or in some other way, he has a purpose in mind for your life.

Henry Blackaby and Claude King

*Trust the LORD your God with all your heart
and lean not on your own understanding;
in all your ways acknowledge him,
and he will make your paths straight.*

Proverbs 3:5-6 NIV

A Prayer for Today

Dear Lord, I am Your creation, and You created
me for a reason. Give me the wisdom to follow
Your direction for my life's journey. Let me do
Your work here on earth by seeking Your will
and living it, knowing that when I trust in You,
Father, I am eternally blessed.

Amen

CHAPTER 14

Searching for Strength

The LORD is my strength and my song . . . .
Exodus 15:2 NIV

God's hand is a never-ending source of strength and courage for those who call upon Him. When we are weary, He gives us power. When we see no hope, God reminds us of His promises. When we grieve, God wipes away our tears. Whatever our circumstances, God will protect us and care for us . . . *if* we let Him.

Have you "tapped in" to the power of God? Have you turned your life and your heart over to Him, or are you muddling along under your own power? The answer to these questions will determine the quality of your life here on earth *and* the destiny of your life throughout all eternity.

The Bible tells us that we can do all things through the power of our risen Savior, Jesus Christ. Our challenge, then, is clear: we must place Christ where He belongs: in *first* place. When we do so, we will surely discover that He offers us the strength to live victoriously in this world *and* eternally in the next.

The same God who empowered Samson,
Gideon, and Paul seeks to empower my life and
your life, because God hasn't changed.

Bill Hybels

Jesus is not a strong man making men and
women who gather around Him weak.
He is the Strong creating the strong.

E. Stanley Jones

Notice what Jesus had to say concerning those
who have wearied themselves by trying to do
things in their own strength: "Come to me,
all you who labor and are heavy laden,
and I will give you rest."

Henry Blackaby and Claude King

God conquers only what we yield to Him.
Yet, when He does, and when our surrender is
complete, He fills us with a new strength that
we could never have known by ourselves.
His conquest is our victory!

Shirley Dobson

Those who hope in the LORD will renew their strength. They will soar on wings like eagles; they will run and not grow weary, they will walk and not be faint.

Isaiah 40:31 NIV

A Prayer for Today

Dear Heavenly Father, You are my strength and my protector. When I am troubled, You comfort me. When I am discouraged, You lift me up. When I am afraid, You deliver me. Let me turn to You, Lord, when I am weak. In times of adversity, let me trust Your plan, Lord, and whatever my circumstances, let me look to You for my strength and my salvation.

Amen

My Thoughts & Prayers
from This Week

My Thoughts & Prayers
for Next Week

CHAPTER 15

Patience and Trust

Therefore humble yourselves under the mighty hand of God, that He may exalt you in due time.

1 Peter 5:6 *NKJV*

We human beings are, by our very nature, impatient. We are impatient with others, impatient with ourselves, and impatient with our Creator. We want things to happen according to our own timetables, but our Heavenly Father may have other plans. That's why we must learn the art of patience.

Psalm 37:7 commands us to "rest in the LORD, and wait patiently for Him" (NKJV). But, for most of us, waiting patiently for Him is difficult. Why? Because we are fallible human beings who seek solutions to our problems today, if not sooner. Still, God instructs us to wait patiently for His plans to unfold, and that's exactly what we should do.

So the next time you find yourself drumming your fingers as you wait for a quick resolution to the challenges of everyday living, take a deep breath and ask God for patience. Be still before your Heavenly Father and trust His timetable: it's the peaceful way to live.

He whose attitude towards Christ is correct
does indeed ask "in His Name" and receives
what he asks for if it is something which does
not stand in the way of his salvation. He gets it,
however, only when he ought to receive it,
for certain things are not refused us,
but their granting is delayed to a fitting time.

St. Augustine

When God's people believe and pray,
the Lord will provide, but we must learn
to wait on him with faithful,
obedient hearts until the answer comes.

Jim Cymbala

God is in no hurry. Compared to the works of
mankind, He is extremely deliberate.
God is not a slave to the human clock.

Charles Swindoll

> *There is a time for everything, and a season for every activity under heaven.*
>
> Ecclesiastes 3:1 NIV

A Prayer for Today

Lord, my sense of timing is fallible and imperfect; Yours is not. Let me trust in Your timetable for my life, and give me the patience and the wisdom to trust *Your* plans, not my own.

Amen

CHAPTER 16

The Steps of a Righteous Man

*But now you must be holy in everything you do,
just as God—who chose you to be his children—
is holy. For he himself has said,
"You must be holy because I am holy."*

1 Peter 1:15-16 NLT

As Christians, we are called to walk with God and obey His commandments. But, we live in a world that presents us with countless temptations to stray far from God's path. We Christians, when confronted with sin, have clear instructions: Walk—or better yet run—in the opposite direction.

When we seek righteousness in our own lives—and when we seek the companionship of those who do likewise—we reap the spiritual rewards that God intends for our lives. When we behave ourselves as godly men and women, we honor God. When we live righteously and according to God's commandments, He blesses us in ways that we cannot fully understand.

Today, take every step of your journey with God as your traveling companion. Read His Word and follow His commandments. Support only those activities that further God's kingdom and your spiritual growth. Be an example of righteous living to your friends, to your neighbors, and to your children. Then, reap the blessings that God has promised to all those who live according to His will and His Word.

The destined end of man is not happiness or health, but holiness. God's one aim is the production of saints. He is not an eternal blessing machine for men; he did not come to save men out of pity; he came to save men because he had created them to be holy.

Oswald Chambers

There is no detour to holiness.
Jesus came to the resurrection through the cross, not around it.

Leighton Ford

Holiness isn't in a style of dress. It's not a matter of rules and regulations. It's a way of life that emanates quietness and rest, joy in family, shared pleasures with friends, the help of a neighbor—and the hope of a Savior.

Joni Eareckson Tada

God's glory is the result of his nature and his actions. He is glorious in his character, for he holds within him everything that is holy, good, and lovely.

C. H. Spurgeon

You will teach me how to live a holy life.
Being with you will fill me with joy;
at your right hand I will find pleasure forever.

Psalm 16:11 NCV

A Prayer for Today

Holy, Holy, Holy . . . You are a righteous and
holy God who commands that I seek to be holy
and righteous. Forgive me when I fall short,
Lord, and renew a right spirit within me.
Let me serve You and obey the teachings of
Your Word. Lead me far from temptation,
Father, and guide me in Your will for my life.

Amen

CHAPTER 17

A Humble Spirit

Yea, all of you be subject one to another,
and be clothed with humility: for God resisteth
the proud, and giveth grace to the humble.
1 Peter 5:5 KJV

ietrich Bonhoeffer observed, "It is very easy to overestimate the importance of our own achievements in comparison with what we owe others." How true. Even those of us who consider ourselves "self-made men" are deeply indebted to more people than we can count. Our first and greatest indebtedness, of course, is to God and His only begotten Son. But we are also indebted to ancestors, parents, teachers, friends, spouses, family members, coworkers, fellow believers . . . and the list goes on.

With so many people who rightfully deserve to share the credit for our successes, how can we gloat? The answer, of course, is that we should not. Proverbs 16:18 warns us that "Pride goes before destruction . . . ." (NIV). And 1 Peter 5:5 teaches us that "God opposes the proud but gives grace to the humble" (NIV).

So, instead of puffing out your chest and saying, "Look at me!", give credit where credit is due, starting with God. And rest assured: There is no such thing as a self-made man. All of us are made by God . . . *He* deserves the glory, not us.

Humility is the fairest and
rarest flower that blooms.

Charles Swindoll

Seeking after God is a two-pronged endeavor.
It requires not only humility to say,
"God, I need you,"
but also a heart that desires
a pure life that is pleasing to the Lord.

Jim Cymbala

Nothing sets a person so much
out of the devil's reach as humility.

Jonathan Edwards

Always be humble, gentle, and patient,
accepting each other in love.

Ephesians 4:2 NCV

A Prayer for Today

Heavenly Father, it is the nature of mankind to be prideful, and I am no exception. When I am boastful, Lord, keep me mindful that all my gifts come from You. When I feel prideful, remind me that You sent Your Son to be a humble carpenter and that Jesus was ridiculed and crucified on a cross. Let me grow beyond my need for earthly praise, God, and let me look only to You for approval. You are the Giver of all things good; let me give all the glory to You.

Amen

CHAPTER 18

Leadership

*We have different gifts,
according to the grace given us . . . .
If it is leadership, let him govern diligently . . . .*
Romans 12:6, 8 NIV

John Maxwell writes, "Great leaders understand that the right attitude will set the right atmosphere, which enables the right response from others." If you are in a position of leadership, whether as a father—or as a leader at your work, your church, or your school—it's up to you to set the right tone by maintaining the right attitude. What's your attitude today? Are you fearful, angry, bored, or worried? Are you confused, bitter, or pessimistic? If so, then you should ask yourself if you're the kind of leader whom you would want to follow. If the answer to that question is no, then it's time to improve your leadership skills.

Our world needs Christian leadership, and so do your family members and coworkers. You can become a trusted, competent, thoughtful leader if you learn to maintain the right attitude: one that is realistic, optimistic, forward looking, and Christ-centered.

It is amazing what will happen in your
leadership when you do not gauge the happiness
of your life or the greatness of your day
by how easy it was.

John Maxwell

When God wants to accomplish something,
He calls dedicated men and women to
challenge His people and lead the way.

Warren Wiersbe

People who inspire others are those who see
invisible bridges at the end of dead-end streets.

Charles Swindoll

Leadership is found in becoming
the servant of all.

Richard Foster

Those who are wise will shine like the brightness of the heavens, and those who lead many to righteousness, like the stars for ever and ever.

Daniel 12:3 NIV

A Prayer for Today

Heavenly Father, when I find myself in
a position of leadership, let me follow
Your teachings and obey Your commandments.
Make me a person of integrity and wisdom,
Lord, and make me a worthy example to those
whom I serve. And, let me turn to You, Lord,
for guidance and for strength in all
that I say and do.

Amen

CHAPTER 19

Discovering Time for Prayer and Meditation

Let the words of my mouth and the meditation of my heart be acceptable in Your sight, O LORD, my strength and my Redeemer.

Psalm 19:14 NKJV

The world seems to grow louder day by day, and our senses seem to be invaded at every turn. But, if we allow the distractions of a clamorous society to separate us from God's peace, we do ourselves a profound disservice. Our task, as dutiful believers, is to carve out moments of silence in a world filled with noise.

If we are to maintain righteous minds and compassionate hearts, we must take time each day for prayer and for meditation. We must make ourselves still in the presence of our Creator. We must quiet our minds and our hearts so that we might sense God's will and His love.

Has the busy pace of life robbed you of the peace that God has promised? If so, it's time to reorder your priorities and your life. Nothing is more important than the time you spend with your Heavenly Father. So be still and claim the inner peace that is found in the silent moments you spend with God.

It takes calm, thoughtful, prayerful meditation
on the Word to extract its deepest nourishment.

Vance Havner

Let your mind soak in the deliverance of God.

Oswald Chambers

Do you want an intimate relationship with
God? If so, you must consistently and faithfully
set aside time so your heavenly Father can
communicate with you through
His Word and His Spirit.

Kay Arthur

I need the spiritual revival that comes from
spending quiet time alone with Jesus in prayer
and in thoughtful meditation on His Word.

Anne Graham Lotz

> *Be still, and know that I am God.*
>
> ↬
>
> Psalm 46:10 KJV

A Prayer for Today

Heavenly Father, in these quiet moments before
this busy day unfolds, I come to You.
May my meditations bring You pleasure just as
surely as they bring me a clearer sense of
Your love and Your peace. May the time
I spend in quiet meditation mold
my day and my life . . . for You.

↬

Amen

CHAPTER 20

Keeping Money in Perspective

Keep your lives free from the love of money,
and be satisfied with what you have.

Hebrews 13:5 NCV

Earthly riches are temporary: here today and soon gone forever. Spiritual riches, on the other hand, are permanent: ours today, ours tomorrow, ours throughout eternity. Yet all too often, we focus our thoughts and energies on the accumulation of earthly treasures, leaving precious little time to accumulate the only treasures that really matter: the spiritual kind.

Our society is in love with money and the things that money can buy. God is not. God cares about people, not possessions, and so must we. We must, to the best of our abilities, love our neighbors as ourselves, and we must, to the best of our abilities, resist the mighty temptation to place possessions ahead of people.

Money, in and of itself, is not evil, but *worshipping* money is. So today, as you prioritize matters of importance for you and yours, remember that God is almighty, but the "almighty" dollar is not.

God is entitled to a portion of our income.
Not because he needs it,
but because we need to give it.

James Dobson

When I have any money,
I get rid of it as quickly as possible,
lest it find a way into my heart.

John Wesley

Servants of God are always more concerned
about ministry than money.

Rick Warren

If a person gets his attitude toward
money straight, it will help straighten out
almost every other area in his life.

Billy Graham

*If riches increase,
do not set your heart upon them.*

⤬

Psalm 62:10 NASB

A Prayer for Today

Dear Lord, help make me a responsible steward
of my financial resources. Let me trust
Your Holy Word, and let me use my tithe for
the support of Your church and
for the eternal glory of Your Son.

⤬

Amen

CHAPTER 21

An Obedient Heart

For this is the love of God,
that we keep his commandments . . . .
1 John 5:3 KJV

How can we demonstrate our love for God? By accepting His Son as our personal Savior and by placing Christ squarely at the center of our lives and our hearts. Jesus said that if we are to love Him, we must obey His commandments (John 14:15). Thus, our obedience to the Master is an expression of our love for Him.

In Ephesians 2:10 we read, "For we are His workmanship, created in Christ Jesus for good works" (NKJV). These words are instructive: We are not saved *by* good works, but *for* good works. Good works are not *the root*, but rather *the fruit* of our salvation.

Today, let the fruits of *your* stewardship be a clear demonstration of your love for Christ. When you do, your good heart will bring forth many good things for yourself and for God. Christ has given you spiritual abundance and eternal life. You, in turn, owe Him good treasure from a single obedient heart: yours.

Success or failure can be pretty well predicted
by the degree to which the heart is fully in it.

John Eldredge

The Christian life is motivated, not by a list of
do's and don'ts, but by the gracious outpouring
of God's love and blessing.

Anne Graham Lotz

Do you wonder where you can go for
encouragement and motivation? Run to Jesus.

Max Lucado

Worship is wonder, love, and praise.
Not only does it cause us to contemplate and
appreciate our holy God, but it gives us vitality,
vigor, and a desire to obey Him.

Franklin Graham

*Jesus answered, "If anyone loves Me,
he will keep My word. My Father will love him,
and We will come to him and
make Our home with him.*

~

John 14:23 HCSB

A Prayer for Today

Heavenly Father, when I turn my thoughts away
from You and Your Word, I suffer. But when
I obey Your commandments, when I place my
faith in You, I am secure. Let me live according
to Your commandments. Direct my path far
from the temptations and distractions of this
world. And, let me discover Your will and
follow it, Dear Lord, this day and always.

~

Amen

My Thoughts & Prayers
from This Week

My Thoughts & Prayers
for Next Week

CHAPTER 22

The Passionate Believer

He did it with all his heart. So he prospered.
2 Chronicles 31:21 NKJV

A re you passionate about your life, your loved ones, your work, and your faith? As a believer who has been saved by a risen Christ, you should be.

As a thoughtful Christian, you have every reason to be enthusiastic about life, but sometimes the struggles of everyday living may cause you to feel decidedly *un*enthusiastic. If you feel that your zest for life is slowly fading away, it's time to slow down, to rest, to count your blessings, and to pray. When you feel worried or weary, you must pray fervently for God to renew your sense of wonderment and excitement.

Life with God is a glorious adventure; revel in it. When you do, God will most certainly smile upon your work *and* your life.

Am I ignitable? God deliver me from the dread asbestos of "other things." Saturate me with the oil of the Spirit that I may be aflame.

Jim Elliot

When we wholeheartedly commit ourselves to God, there is nothing mediocre or run-of-the-mill about us. To live for Christ is to be passionate about our Lord and about our lives.

Jim Gallery

If I should neglect prayer but a single day, I should lose a great deal of the fire of faith.

Martin Luther

It's ironic that one of the best remedies for impending burnout is to give yourself away— to pick out one time and place each week where you can stretch out your hands for the pure joy of doing it.

Liz Curtis Higgs

Never be lacking in zeal,
but keep your spiritual fervor, serving the Lord.

Romans 12:11 NIV

A Prayer for Today

Lord, let me find my strength in You.
When I am weary, give me rest. When I feel
overwhelmed, let me look to You for
my priorities. Let Your passion be my passion,
Lord, and let Your way be my way,
today and forever.

Amen

CHAPTER 23

The Power of Perseverance

Let endurance have its perfect result,
so that you may be perfect and complete,
lacking in nothing.

James 1:4 NASB

As you travel along life's roads, you'll encounter your fair share of roadblocks and stumbling blocks; these situations require courage, patience, and above all, perseverance. As an example of perfect perseverance, we Christians need look no further than our Savior, Jesus Christ.

Jesus finished what He began. Despite the torture He endured, despite the shame of the cross, Jesus was steadfast in His faithfulness to God. We, too, must remain faithful, especially during times of hardship.

Perhaps you are in a hurry for God to reveal His plans for your life. If so, be forewarned: God operates on His own timetable, not yours. Sometimes, God may answer your prayers with silence, and when He does, you must patiently persevere. In times of trouble, you must remain steadfast and trust in the merciful goodness of your Heavenly Father. Whatever your problem, He can handle it. Your job is to keep persevering until He does.

As we find that it is not easy to persevere
in this being "alone with God," we begin to
realize that it is because we are not "wholly for
God." God has a right to demand that
He should have us completely for Himself.

Andrew Murray

Jesus taught that perseverance is
the essential element in prayer.

E. M. Bounds

All rising to a great place is by a winding stair.

Francis Bacon

God never gives up on you,
so don't you ever give up on Him.

Marie T. Freeman

For you have need of endurance,
so that after you have done the will of God,
you may receive the promise.

⌒

Hebrews 10:36 NKJV

A Prayer for Today

Heavenly Father, sometimes, this life is difficult
indeed. Sometimes, I am fearful. Sometimes,
I cry tears of bitterness and loss, but even then,
You never leave my side. Today, Lord, let me be
a finisher of my faith. Let me persevere—
even if the day is difficult—and let me follow
Your Son Jesus this day and forever.

⌒

Amen

CHAPTER 24

Beyond Worry

Let not your heart be troubled;
you believe in God, believe also in Me.

John 14:1 NKJV

I f you are a man with lots of obligations and plenty of responsibilities, it is simply a fact of life: You worry. From time to time, you worry about health, about finances, about safety, about family, and about countless other concerns, some great and some small.

Where is the best place to take your worries? Take them to God. Take your troubles to Him; take your fears to Him; take your doubts to Him; take your weaknesses to Him; take your sorrows to Him . . . and leave them all there. Seek protection from the One who offers you eternal salvation; build your spiritual house upon the Rock that cannot be moved.

Perhaps you are uncertain about your future or your finances—or perhaps you are simply a "worrier" by nature. If so, it's time to focus *less* on your troubles and *more* on God's promises. And that's as it should be because God is trustworthy . . . and you are protected.

The beginning of anxiety is the end of faith,
and the beginning of true faith is
the end of anxiety.

George Mueller

Don't let worry rob you of the joy that is
rightfully yours. God is in heaven, and
He knows your every need. Focus on God and
His provisions, and watch gratefully as
the worries of today begin to fade away.

Jim Gallery

God uses every cloud which comes in our
physical life, in our moral or spiritual life,
or in our circumstances, to bring us nearer to
him until we come to the place where our Lord
Jesus Christ lived, and we do not allow
our hearts to be troubled.

Oswald Chambers

The closer you live to God,
the smaller everything else appears.

Rick Warren

Therefore I tell you, do not worry about your life, what you will eat or drink; or about your body, what you will wear. Is not life more important than food, and the body more important than clothes? Look at the birds of the air; they do not sow or reap or store away in barns, and yet your heavenly Father feeds them. Are you not much more valuable than they?

Matthew 6:25-27 NIV

A Prayer for Today

Forgive me, Lord, when I worry. Worry reflects a lack of trust in Your ability to meet my every need. Help me to work, Lord, and not to worry. And, keep me mindful, Father, that nothing, absolutely nothing, will happen this day that You and I cannot handle together.

Amen

CHAPTER 25

Real Repentance

*If we confess our sins, He is faithful and righteous
to forgive us our sins and to cleanse us
from all unrighteousness.*

1 John 1:9 NASB

Who among us has sinned? All of us. But, God calls upon us to turn away from sin by following His commandments. And the good news is this: When we do ask God's forgiveness and turn our hearts to Him, He forgives us absolutely and completely.

Genuine repentance requires more than simply offering God apologies for our misdeeds. Real repentance may *start* with feelings of sorrow and remorse, but it *ends* only when we turn away from the sin that has heretofore distanced us from our Creator. In truth, we offer our most meaningful apologies to God, not with our words, but with our actions. As long as we are still engaged in sin, we may be "repenting," but we have not fully "repented."

Is there an aspect of your life that is distancing you from your God? If so, ask for His forgiveness, and—just as importantly—stop sinning. Then, wrap yourself in the protection of God's Word. When you do, you will be secure.

Repentance is among other things a sincere apology to God for distrusting Him so long, and faith is throwing oneself upon Christ in complete confidence.

A. W. Tozer

When true repentance comes, God will not hesitate for a moment to forgive, cast the sins in the sea of forgetfulness, and put the child on the road to restoration.

Beth Moore

The pardon of God deletes past, present, and future sins—completely!

Franklin Graham

Repentance is an inward conviction that expresses itself in an outward action.

Max Lucado

*If My people who are called by My name will
humble themselves, and pray and seek My face,
and turn from their wicked ways,
then I will hear from heaven,
and will forgive their sin and heal their land.*

2 Chronicles 7:14 NKJV

A Prayer for Today

When I stray from Your commandments, Lord,
I must not only confess my sins, I must also
turn from them. When I fall short, help me to
change. When I reject Your Word and Your will
for my life, guide me back to Your side. Forgive
my sins, Dear Lord, and help me live according
to Your plan for my life. Your plan is perfect,
Father; I am not. Let me trust in You.

Amen

CHAPTER 26

Seeking God

The LORD is good to those whose hope is in him, to the one who seeks him.

Lamentations 3:25 NIV

The instructions of Matthew 6:33 are clear: "But seek first the kingdom of God and His righteousness, and all these things shall be added to you" (NKJV). And, when we genuinely seek God—with our hearts open and our prayers lifted—we need not look far because God is with us always.

Sometimes, in the crush of our daily duties, God may seem far away, but He is not. God is everywhere we have ever been and everywhere we will ever go. He is with us night and day; He knows our thoughts and our prayers. And, when we earnestly seek Him, we will find Him because He is here, waiting patiently for us to reach out to Him.

Today, let us reach out to the Giver of all blessings. Let us turn to Him for guidance and for strength. Today, may we, who have been given so much, seek God and invite Him into every aspect of our lives. And, let us remember that no matter our circumstances, God never leaves us; He is here . . . always right here.

There is nothing on earth that can satisfy our
deepest longing. We long to see God.
The leaves of life are rustling with the rumor
that we will—and we won't be satisfied
until we do.

Max Lucado

Let us humble our hearts before the Lord and
seek his help and approval above
all other things.

Jim Cymbala

Our souls were made to live in an upper
atmosphere, and we stifle and choke if we live
on any lower level. Our eyes were made to look
off from these heavenly heights, and
our vision is distorted by any lower gazing.

Hannah Whitall Smith

Time spent in seeking the Holy Spirit is
the most fruitful time of one's life.

E. Stanley Jones

*And without faith it is impossible to please God,
because anyone who comes to him must believe
that he exists and that he rewards those who
earnestly seek him.*

Hebrews 11:6 NIV

A Prayer for Today

How comforting it is, Dear Lord, to know that
if I seek You, I will find You. You are with me,
Father, every step that I take. Let me reach out
to You, and let me praise You for revealing
Your Word, Your way, and Your love.

Amen

CHAPTER 27

God's Sovereignty

You shall have no other gods before Me.

Exodus 20:3 NKJV

God is sovereign: He reigns over all His creation, including You. Your challenge is to recognize God's sovereignty and live in accordance with His commandments. As you prayerfully consider the path that God intends for you to take, here are things you should do: You should study His Word and be ever watchful for His signs. You should associate with fellow believers who will encourage your spiritual growth. You should listen carefully to that inner voice that speaks to you in the quiet moments of your daily devotionals. And, as you continually seek God's unfolding purpose for your life, you should be patient.

Your Heavenly Father may not always reveal himself as quickly as you would like. But rest assured: God is sovereign, God is here, God is love, and God intends to use you in wonderful, unexpected ways. He desires to lead you along a path of His choosing. Your challenge is to watch, to listen, to learn . . . and to follow.

God has charged Himself with full responsibility
for our eternal happiness and stands ready to
take over the management of our lives
the moment we turn in faith to Him.

A. W. Tozer

We do not understand the intricate pattern of
the stars in their course, but we know that
He who created them does, and that just as
surely as He guides them, He is charting
a safe course for us.

Billy Graham

Nothing happens by happenstance.
I am not in the hands of fate, nor am I
the victim of man's whims or the devil's ploys.
There is One who sits above man, above Satan,
and above all heavenly hosts as
the ultimate authority of all the universe.
That One is my God and my Father!

Kay Arthur

*The true children of God are those who
let God's Spirit lead them.*

〜

Romans 8:14 NCV

A Prayer for Today

Dear Lord, I am Your creation, and You created
me for a reason. Give me the wisdom to follow
Your direction for my life's journey, and give
our leaders the wisdom to direct our nation
according to Your infinite wisdom and
Your perfect will. Lead us, Father, and let us
trust You completely, today and forever.

〜

Amen

CHAPTER 28

Protection from Temptation

No temptation has seized you except what is
common to man. And God is faithful;
he will not let you be tempted beyond what
you can bear. But when you are tempted,
he will also provide a way out so that
you can stand up under it.

1 Corinthians 10:13 NIV

B ecause our world is filled with temptations, we confront them at every turn. Some of these temptations are small—eating a second piece of chocolate cake, for example. Too much cake may cause us to defile, at least in a modest way, the bodily temple that God has entrusted to our care. But two pieces of cake will not bring us to our knees. Other temptations, however, are not so harmless.

The devil, it seems, is working overtime these days, and causing pain and heartache in more places and in more ways than ever before. We, as Christians, must remain vigilant. Not only must we resist Satan when he confronts us, but we must also avoid those places where Satan can most easily tempt us. And, if we are to avoid the unending temptations of this world, we must arm ourselves with the Word of God.

In a letter to believers, Peter offered a stern warning: "Your adversary, the devil, prowls around like a roaring lion, seeking someone to devour" (1 Peter 5:8 NASB). What was true in New Testament times is equally true in our own. Satan tempts his prey and then devours them. As believing Christians, we must beware. And, if we seek righteousness in our own lives, we must earnestly wrap ourselves in the protection of God's Holy Word. When we do, we are secure.

Some temptations come to the industrious,
but all temptations attack the idle.

C. H. Spurgeon

A man who gives in to temptation after five
minutes simply does not know
what it would have been like an hour later.

C. S. Lewis

Rebuke the Enemy in your own name and
he laughs; command him in the name
of Christ and he flees.

John Eldredge

It is easier to stay out of temptation
than to get out of it.

Rick Warren

*The Lord knows how to deliver
the godly out of temptations.*

2 Peter 2:9 NKJV

A Prayer for Today

Dear Lord, this world is filled with temptations, distractions, and frustrations. When I turn my thoughts away from You and Your Word, Lord, I suffer bitter consequences. But, when I trust in Your commandments, I am safe. Direct my path far from the temptations and distractions of the world. Let me discover Your will and follow it, Dear Lord, this day and always.

Amen

My Thoughts & Prayers
from This Week

_____

_____

_____

_____

_____

_____

_____

_____

_____

_____

_____

_____

_____

_____

_____

_____

_____

_____

_____

_____

_____

_____

_____

My Thoughts & Prayers
for Next Week

_____

_____

_____

_____

_____

_____

_____

_____

_____

_____

_____

_____

_____

_____

_____

_____

_____

_____

_____

_____

_____

_____

CHAPTER 29

Sharing the Good News

But ye shall receive power, after that
the Holy Ghost is come upon you: and ye shall
be witnesses unto me both in Jerusalem,
and in all Judea, and in Samaria,
and unto the uttermost part of the earth.

Acts 1:8 KJV

One way that we demonstrate our love for others is by sharing the Good News of Jesus Christ. The story of Jesus should be shouted from the rooftops by believers the world over. But all too often, it is not. For a variety of reasons, too many Christians keep their beliefs to themselves, and when they do, the world suffers because of their failure to speak up.

Paul offered a message to believers of every generation when he wrote, "God has not given us a spirit of timidity" (2 Timothy 1:7 NASB). Paul's meaning is straightforward: When sharing our testimonies, we must be courageous, forthright, and unashamed.

Billy Graham observed, "Our faith grows by expression. If we want to keep our faith, we must share it." If you are a follower of Christ, the time to express your belief in Him is now. You know how He has touched your heart; help Him do the same for others.

The evangelistic harvest is always urgent.
The destiny of men and of nations is always
being decided. Every generation is strategic. We
are not responsible for the past generation, and
we cannot bear the full responsibility for the
next one, but we do have our generation. God
will hold us responsible as to how well we
fulfill our responsibilities to this age and
take advantage of our opportunities.

Billy Graham

Jesus' images portray the Kingdom as a kind
of secret force. Sheep among wolves, treasure
hidden in a field, the tiniest seed in a garden,
wheat growing among weeds, a pinch of yeast
worked into bread dough; all these hint at
a movement that works within society,
changing it from inside out.

Philip Yancey

There is too much sermonizing and
too little witnessing. People do not come to
Christ at the end of an argument.

Vance Havner

*You're here to be light, bringing out
the God-colors in the world. God is not a secret
to be kept. We're going public with this,
as public as a city on a hill. If I make you
light-bearers, you don't think I'm going to hide
you under a bucket, do you? I'm putting you
on a lightstand. Now that I've put you there on
a hilltop, on a lightstand, shine! Keep open house;
be generous with your lives. By opening up
to others, you'll prompt people to open up
with God, this generous Father in heaven.*

Matthew 5:14-16 MSG

A Prayer for Today

Dear Lord, the life that I live and the words
that I speak bear witness to my faith.
Make me a faithful servant of Your Son,
and let my testimony be worthy of You.
Let my words be sure and true, Lord,
and let my actions point others to You.

Amen

CHAPTER 30

The Value of Hard Work

. . . I worked harder than all of them—yet not I,
but the grace of God that was with me.

1 Corinthians 15:10 NIV

God's Word teaches us the value of hard work. In his second letter to the Thessalonians, Paul warns, ". . . if any would not work, neither should he eat" (3:10 KJV). And the Book of Proverbs proclaims, "One who is slack in his work is brother to one who destroys" (18:9 NIV). In short, God has created a world in which diligence is rewarded, but sloth is not. So, whatever it is that you choose to do, do it with commitment, excitement, and vigor.

Hard work is not simply a proven way to get ahead; it's also part of God's plan for you. God did not create you for a life of mediocrity; He created you for far greater things. Reaching for greater things usually requires work and lots of it, which is perfectly fine with God. After all, He knows that you're up to the task, and He has big plans for you if you possess a loving heart and willing hands.

Thank God every morning when you get up
that you have something which must be done,
whether you like it or not. Work breeds
a hundred virtues that idleness never knows.

Charles Kingsley

The world does not consider labor a blessing;
therefore it flees and hates it, but the pious who
fear the Lord labor with a ready and
cheerful heart, for they know God's command,
and they acknowledge His calling.

Martin Luther

Wouldn't it make astounding difference,
not only in the quality of the work we do,
but also in the satisfaction, even our joy,
if we recognized God's gracious gift
in every single task?

Elisabeth Elliot

True willpower and courage are not on
the battlefield, but in everyday conquests
over our inertia, laziness, and boredom.

D. L. Moody

Each will receive his own reward according to his own labor . . . .
Each man's work will become evident.

~

1 Corinthians 3:8, 13 NASB

A Prayer for Today

Lord, I know that You desire a bountiful harvest for all Your children. But, You have instructed us that we must sow before we reap, not after. Help me, Lord, to sow the seeds of Your abundance everywhere I go. Let me be diligent in all my undertakings and give me patience to wait for Your harvest. In time, Lord, let me reap the harvest that is found in Your will for my life.

~

Amen

CHAPTER 31

The Ultimate Power, The Ultimate Love

For God hath not given us the spirit of fear;
but of power, and of love, and of a sound mind.

2 Timothy 1:7 KJV

God's power is not burdened by boundaries or by limitations—and neither, for that matter, is His love. The love that flows from the heart of God is infinite—and today offers yet another opportunity to celebrate that love.

Have you made God the cornerstone of your life, or is He relegated to a few hours on Sunday morning? Have you genuinely allowed God to reign over every corner of your heart, or have you attempted to place Him in a spiritual compartment? The answer to these questions will determine the direction of your day *and* the direction of your life.

God's love for you is deeper and more profound than you can fathom. In times of trouble, He will comfort you; in times of sorrow, He will dry your tears. When you are weak or sorrowful, God is as near as your next breath. He stands at the door of your heart and waits. Welcome Him in and allow Him to rule. And then, accept the peace and the power and the protection and the abundance that only God can give.

Nothing is more powerful than a surrendered
life in the hands of God.

Rick Warren

Prayer imparts the power to walk and not faint.

Oswald Chambers

Today God's eyes are still running all across
America . . . the world . . . looking for someone,
anyone, who will totally and passionately seek
him, who is determined that every thought and
action will be pleasing in his sight. For such
a person or group, God will prove himself
mighty. His power will explode on their behalf.

Jim Cymbala

The amount of power you experience to live
a victorious, triumphant Christian life is
directly proportional to the freedom you give
the Spirit to be Lord of your life!

Anne Graham Lotz

Let every soul be subject unto the higher powers.
For there is no power but of God:
the powers that be are ordained of God.

~

Romans 13:1 KJV

A Prayer for Today

Dear Lord, You have the power to make all
things new. When I grow weary, let me turn
my thoughts and my prayers to You. When I am
discouraged, restore my faith in You.
Renew my strength, Father, and let me draw
comfort and courage from Your promises and
from Your unending love.

~

Amen

My Thoughts & Prayers
for the Month

My Thoughts & Prayers
for the Month

Bible Verses
to Consider

Abundance

And God will generously provide all you need.
Then you will always have everything you need and
plenty left over to share with others.

2 Corinthians 9:8 NLT

Until now you have asked for nothing in My name.
Ask and you will receive,
that your joy may be complete.

John 16:24 HCSB

Misfortune pursues the sinner,
but prosperity is the reward of the righteous.

Proverbs 13:21 NIV

My cup runs over. Surely goodness and mercy
shall follow me all the days of my life;
and I will dwell in the house of the LORD forever.

Psalm 23:5-6 NKJV

I have come that they may have life, and that they may have it more abundantly.

John 10:10 NKJV

Courage

*Be strong and of good courage, and do it;
do not fear nor be dismayed, for the LORD God—
my God—will be with you. He will not leave you
nor forsake you, until you have finished all the work
for the service of the house of the LORD.*

1 Chronicles 28:20 NKJV

*But He said to them, "Why are you fearful,
you of little faith?" Then He got up and rebuked
the winds and the sea. And there was a great calm.*

Matthew 8:26 HCSB

*Peace I leave with you, my peace I give unto you:
not as the world giveth, give I unto you.
Let not your heart be troubled,
neither let it be afraid.*

John 14:27 KJV

*Have I not commanded you? Be strong and
of good courage; do not be afraid, nor be dismayed,
for the LORD your God is with you
wherever you go.*

Joshua 1:9 NKJV

Do not be afraid...

I am your shield,

your very great reward.

Genesis 15:1 NIV

Faith

The Good News shows how God makes people right with himself—that it begins and ends with faith. As the Scripture says, "But those who are right with God will live by trusting in him."

Romans 1:17 NCV

Be on the alert, stand firm in the faith, act like men, be strong.

1 Corinthians 16:13 NASB

But he must ask in faith without any doubting, for the one who doubts is like the surf of the sea, driven and tossed by the wind.

James 1:6 NASB

Now without faith it is impossible to please God, for the one who draws near to Him must believe that He exists and rewards those who seek Him.

Hebrews 11:6 HCSB

The righteous will live by his faith.

Habakkuk 2:4 NIV

Service

*His master replied, "Well done, good and faithful
servant! You have been faithful with a few things;
I will put you in charge of many things.
Come and share your master's happiness!"*

Matthew 25:21 NIV

*Then the righteous will answer Him, saying,
"Lord, when did we see You hungry and feed You,
or thirsty and give You drink? When did we see You
a stranger and take You in, or naked and clothe
You? Or when did we see You sick, or in prison,
and come to You?" And the King will answer and
say to them, "Assuredly, I say to you, inasmuch as
you did it to one of the least of these My brethren,
you did it to Me."*

Matthew 25:37-40 NKJV

*If anyone serves Me, let him follow Me;
and where I am, there My servant will be also.
If anyone serves Me, him My Father will honor.*

John 12:26 NKJV

But he who is greatest among you shall be your servant.

Matthew 23:11 NKJV

Wisdom

*But the wisdom that is from above is first pure,
then peaceable, gentle, willing to yield,
full of mercy and good fruits, without partiality and
without hypocrisy.*

James 3:17 NKJV

*Do not deceive yourselves. If any one of you thinks
he is wise by the standards of this age, he should
become a "fool" so that he may become wise.
For the wisdom of this world is foolishness
in God's sight.*

1 Corinthians 3:18-19 NIV

*Trust in the LORD with all thine heart;
and lean not unto thine own understanding.
In all thy ways acknowledge him,
and he shall direct thy paths.*

Proverbs 3:5-6 KJV

*Those who are wise will shine like the brightness
of the heavens, and those who lead many to
righteousness, like the stars for ever and ever.*

Daniel 12:3 NIV

Happy is the man who
finds wisdom,
and the man who
gains understanding.

Proverbs 3:13 NKJV